Cowgirl Annie's Wild Ride

By
Cowgirl Annie

D1526497

Illustrated by
Daboin Edwin

Cowgirl Annie started her day like all others.
She ate breakfast, fed the chickens,

caught her pony, Puff, and rode to school with her siblings.
Their mom yelled as they left the barnyard,
"Don't you run the horses in this heat."

When school was over, Cowgirl Annie ran to the barn to catch Puff for the ride home. Puff refused to let her put the bridle on him. He put his nose on the ground.
He turned his head to the right, and then he lifted it so high that she couldn't reach his mouth

Cowgirl Annie asked her sister to help her, but Terri said,
"You bridled him this morning. You can do it now."
Then she rode off with Joel and Vonna.

Mad about the lack of help,
Cowgirl Annie pulled her hat
down low, crawled up the
fence,
and climbed on Puff
without a bridle.

She reached out and unlatched the gate. Then she gave it a mighty kick open.

Puff bolted through the gate and across the school yard.
"YAHOO!" yelled Cowgirl Annie.

He darted around the corner of the schoolhouse,
almost unseating Cowgirl Annie, so she grabbed a handful of mane
and hung on as he cut sharply around the corner fence post.

Wanting to catch up with the other horses, Puff raced down the path.

Cowgirl Annie had to cover her face to keep from being slapped by willows just before Puff plunged into the creek, splashing her with mud and water.

He galloped under a tree with branches so low that
Cowgirl Annie had to lie flat against his neck to get under them

Puff caught up with the siblings, and Cowgirl Annie waved as she flew by them.
"You're not supposed to be running," they called.
"I can't stop him," she replied.

Cowgirl Annie's eyes grew wide when she saw the wire gate lying open across the path. Worried that Puff wouldn't see the gate, she yelled, "WHOA!" Puff ran faster. She squeezed tightly with her legs as she felt Puff gather himself up, jump high over the gate, and continue galloping.

When they approached the deep, scary washout, Cowgirl Annie tried to get Puff to go up on the road and around it, but he wouldn't. Helpless and scared of dying, Cowgirl Annie closed her eyes. As Puff's hooves pounded close to the edge, she prayed that the path wouldn't cave off and cause them to fall into the deep, dark hole.

When she opened her eyes, she saw they were safely past the dangerous washout, and she thanked God. The corner post into the hayfield was coming up next. It was a large post wrapped in barbed wire.

Cowgirl Annie was always afraid that she might get her leg cut on it. As Puff went around the corner, she had to lift her leg up to keep it away from the wire.

When they reached the hayfield, Puff came to a sudden halt,
sending Cowgirl Annie flying over his head into the dirt.
He hadn't eaten all day, and he was hungry.

While Puff was eating grass, Cowgirl Annie
threw her leg over his neck and crawled up onto his back.

Puff was starving and continued munching his way across the hayfield while Cowgirl Annie kicked his sides and spanked his rump.

Cowgirl Annie was exhausted when they finally made it across the hayfield.
She decided to take a nap on Puff while waiting at the
gate for her brother and sisters.

When they caught up, Terri said,
"Well, I guess I could put the bridle on for you."
However, when Puff saw the open gate, he took off like a shot.

He charged through the flock of sheep, scattering lambs everywhere.

He sent the baby calves bucking and running as he passed by them.

When they got to the corral, Cowgirl Annie slid off, relieved that the wild ride had ended.

She put Puff in the corral and ran to the house hollering, "Mom! Guess what I did?"

Her mom took one look at Cowgirl Annie and gasped, "I don't know what you did, but you look like you just rode a tornado home."

The End

Text and Illustrations copyright © 2019 by Angela Lytle

Published by Lazy 2 Y Publishing

Wall SD 57790

For orders please e-mail angelalytle50@gmail.com

All rights reserved.

No part of this publication may be reproduced, distributed, or transmitted in any form or by any means, including photocopying,

recording, or other electronic or mechanical methods, without the prior written permission of the publisher. Except in the case of brief quotations embodied in reviews and certain other noncommercial uses permitted by copyright laws. The moral right of the author and illustrator has been asserted. Cover design and illustrations by Daboin Edwin

Book Formatting by FormattedBooks.com

Hardback ISBN-978-1-7322569-0-3

Paperback ISBN-978-1-7322569-1-0

eBook ISBN-978-1-7322569-2-7

Library of Congress Control Number: #2018965370

AUTHOR DEDICATION

To my husband Rusty, Thank you for loving me.
To my sister Terri, Thank you for the wild ride
I took on Dawn so long ago.

About the Author

Angela Lytle chose to use Cowgirl Annie as her penname. She grew up on a ranch in South Dakota with her six siblings. She continues the ranching lifestyle with her husband, Rusty, and their 4 boys. She was active in 4-H, Future Farmers of America, and rodeo. She enjoys gardening, cooking, quilting and riding. Her love of kids led her to be a 4-H leader for over 20 years. She decided to embark on a new adventure writing children's books, while waiting for grandkids to enter her life. BRING ON THE KIDS!

Fun Facts

Angela rode horses three miles to the Elk Vale School for eight years. The school had an old barn where the students kept the horses while they were in school. The school never had indoor plumbing, so the families took turns bringing water to drink and for washing up when needed. Angela's dad and grandpa also attended school at Elk Vale. It was a one room country school built in 1889.

Angela was 9 years old that day when she had to ride home without a bridle. She didn't fall off that day, but she thought it made the story more interesting.

SELF-PUBLISHING
SCHOOL

NOW IT'S YOUR TURN

Discover the EXACT 3-step blueprint you need to become a bestselling author in 3 months.

Self-Publishing School helped me, and now I want them to help you with this FREE WEBINAR!

Even if you're busy, bad at writing, or don't know where to start, you CAN write a bestseller and build your best life.

With tools and experience across a variety niches and professions, Self-Publishing School is the only resource you need to take your book to the finish line!

DON'T WAIT

Watch this FREE WEBINAR now, and
Say "YES" to becoming a bestseller:

https://xe172.isrefer.com/go/affegwebinar/bookbrosinc6436/

Made in the USA
Monee, IL
22 September 2020

42281856R00021